CU00793908

POCKET IMAGES

Gareloch
& Rosneath
Peninsula

Historical Note

" Heirloom of red Flodden's glory ! guarded through so many ages,
From thy tranquil happy story, men may fill enchanted pages—
From the times when all these regions heard the sound of Norway's galleys,
And the Maiden Monarch's legions saved the land in yonder valleys :
Legends tell how noble Wallace here awhile his destined sorrow
Baffled, ere o'er wrong and malice dawned his country's happier morrow.
Read the Blind Bard's rough recital ! How Rosneath's tall castle slumbered
When he dealt his foes requital, and these shores with dead were cumbered.
It had seen beneath its rafter, king, and soldier, and crusader ;
Freed from alien bonds thereafter, never hither, came invader."

Rosneath has a great place in Scottish history. In 1489, the lands of Rosneath were conveyed by Royal gift to Colin, First Earl of Argyll, and thereafter the Estates were handed down in succession through the centuries. Archibald, the second Earl, was killed at the Battle of Flodden, along with his brother-in-law, the Earl of Lennox. Archibald, the eighth Earl and the first Marquis of Argyll, raised an army to oppose the Marquis of Huntly, who had hoisted the standard of rebellion, and was actively engaged in hostilities throughout Scotland till defeated at the Battle of Inverlochy by Montrose, when some 1,500 of his followers were killed. The family fortunes revived, and at the Coronation of the King at Scone in 1651, Argyll placed the Crown on King Charles' head. His services were ill-requited, and he was beheaded in Edinburgh in 1661. Thereafter, the Argylls served Scotland as soldiers, statesmen and diplomats, and in recent years the Estate was the summer residence of her Royal Highness Princess Louise, Duchess of Argyll. At one time, the only houses on the shore were the Ferry House and a few cottages, near where the Cove Pier now stands, close to the landing place described by Sir Walter Scott in the " Heart of Midlothian " as " Cairds Cove." The charm of the winding bays and the beauty of the scenery soon led to extensive feuing, and now there are many lovely well-wooded residences along the Eastern shore. An important part of the Estate was requisitioned by the Admiralty, and the Army took over the Castle and Policies, which are now in the process of being de-requisitioned. It is of historical interest that the plans for The North African Combined British-American Landing were made at Rosneath Castle.

All royalties from the sales of this book
will be donated to the
Children's Hospice Association Scotland (CHAS)
Registered Charity No. 136410

POCKET IMAGES

Gareloch & Rosneath Peninsula

Keith Hall

NONSUCH

Gareloch in the 1930s.

First published 2000
This new pocket edition 2007
Images unchanged from first edition

Nonsuch Publishing Limited
Cirencester Road, Chalford,
Stroud, Gloucestershire, GL6 8PE
www.nonsuch-publishing.com

Nonsuch Publishing is an imprint of NPI Media Group

British Library Cataloguing in Publication Data.
A catalogue record for this book is available from the British Library.

ISBN 978-1-84588-402-4

Typesetting and origination by Nonsuch Publishing Limited
Printed in Great Britain by Oaklands Book Services Limited

Contents

Children's Hospice Association Scotland   6

Acknowledgments   7

Bibliography   7

Introduction   8

Gareloch   9

Garelochhead to Coulport   57

Children's Hospice Association Scotland

The Children's Hospice Association Scotland (CHAS) is a Scottish charity established in 1992 by a small group of parents and professionals who understood the needs of children with life-limiting conditions and their families. Rachel House, Scotland's first children's hospice, is run by CHAS. Opened in 1996, it supports families throughout Scotland by providing:

> Specialist palliative support through respite care and emergency care for children with life-limiting, life-threatening and terminal conditions.

> Short term breaks for children and their families.

> Terminal care and bereavement counselling.

> Friendship, information, advice and practical support for families, with support offered in their own homes at times of special stress.

There are an estimated 1,200 children in Scotland who have a life-limiting condition. Sadly, the demand is growing for the services that only a children's hospice can offer, and CHAS is currently serching for a site for its second children's hospice, which, this time, will be built in the West of Scotland.

CHAS thanks the author for generously donating all the royalties from the sales of this book.

Morag Rhodes
PA/CHAS Co-ordinator

Acknowledgments

I would like to thank the following people for their help and assistance in compiling this book: Mr P. McCann and his staff at the Helensburgh Library, particularly Mrs E. Harris; the Rosneath Residents and Tenants Association for their encouragement and friendly advice.

I am also very grateful to the following for the loan of their photographs and their recollections: Mr and Mrs D. Royal; Mrs M. McMorran; Mr and Mrs D. Flemming; Mr and Mrs D. Payne; Mr C. Anderson; Mr E. Montgomery.

I also wish to thank countless other people who have patiently answered my numerous questions and shared with me their photographs and memories. Finally, I ask forgiveness of any contributors who may have been inadvertently omitted from these acknowledgments.

Bibliography

The Book of Dumbartenshire, Vol. II, Irving, 1879
The Call of the Island, C.L. Warr
The Glimmering Landscape, C.L. Warr
History of Dumbartenshire, Irving, 1924
Annals of Garelochside, W.C. Maughan, 1897
First Statistical Account of Scotland
Second Statistical Account of Scotland
Third Statistical Account of Scotland, 1959
The Isle of Rosneath, F.M. Crum, 1948
Helensburgh Advertiser
The West Highland Railway, J. Thomas, 1965
United States Navy Base Two, D. Royal, 2000

Introduction

... Apart from enjoying the book and stirring memories, I hope it might encourage some readers to delve into their old pictures and share them, for now such pictures are indeed the 'keepers of the past'...

I would like to think that this book is a direct result of that plea, which appeared in a earlier book about Rosneath. Nothing evokes nostalgia like old photographs: they can stir and elicit memories in a unique and potent way, and, as a result, there probably is no better generation bridge. Some of the pictures in this book, may I be so bold as to suggest, might be historically significant, but all of them are charming. Long may these old photographs continue to surface from their resting places in dusty drawers and timeworn albums and I look forward to produce more books on Gareloch.

It is not possible, and, indeed, it may not be desirable in a book of this type, to fully tell the rich and varied history of the area, but if this book encourages some readers to go away and further explore their local history, then I am sure they will find it a rewarding and satisfying exercise.

Whether we are newcomers to the area or our families have lived here for generations, this area is our home and its past is now ours. The stories of Princess Louise, the echo at Camsail Bay, the 'White Lady' ghost, who is said to haunt the Yew tree Avenue, are all now part of our collective past, and just maybe, as such, we have some collective responsibility for the custody of the memories.

'This place is beautiful beyond my picturing of it'.
John McLeod Campbell.

Keith Hall
Clynder
August 2000

Gareloch

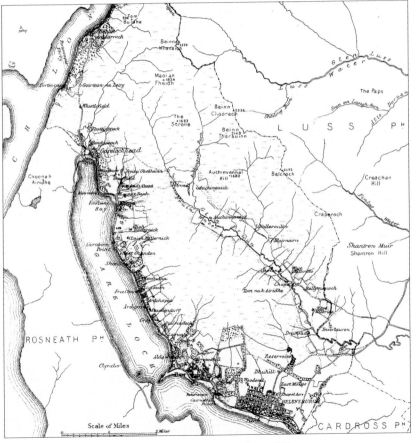

A map of the old Row parish. The spelling was change to Rhu in 1927.

Ardencaple Castle

Valentines Series

Ardencarple Castle, the ancestral home of the clan MacAulay. The lands were originally in the possession of the Earls of Lennox, who, in 1200, granted the land to Aulay, a younger son of the family. In time the lands of the Ardencarple Lairds extended from Garelochhead in the north to Cardross and across to Glen Fruin.

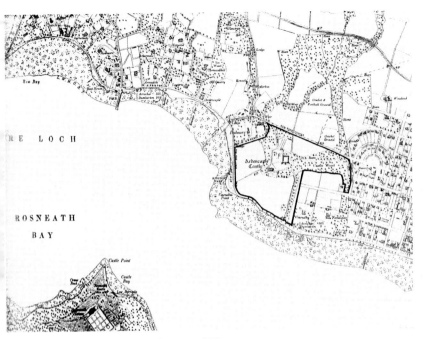

This map shows the much-reduced estate in 1929.

The castle in a postcard dating from the 1900s.

The castle in 1926. The massive retaining wall can still be seen, as can the tower in the naval married quarters estate.

Above and below: Views of the castle from the gardens.

The entrance hall of the castle.

The castle's writing room with original furniture and fireplace. The window looked out on to the Clyde.

The wood-panelled dining room.

The elegant drawing room.

Above: Ardencarple Castle Lodge, the castle's gate house. On the left of the picture, the castle can be seen. An estate can be seen being constructed.

Left: The end of the castle: after much discussion the castle was finally demolished in 1958.

Opposite above: The village of Rhu.

Opposite below: A view from Ardenconnel Woods across the Gareloch to the Rosneath Peninsular. The training ship *Empress* can be seen in the loch.

Gareloch from Ardenconnel Road

In this view, looking down Ardenconnel Road towards the Loch, the *Empress*, an ex-Royal Navy warship (HMS *Revenge*), can be seen through the trees. The ship was effectively a floating reform school that could cater for up to 400 boys, and she was paid for by several leading Glasgow businessmen. She replaced the Cumberland, which had been moved to the loch for this purpose in 1897. This first ship lasted until 1889, when, allegedly, she was set alight by some of the boys.

The village from the foreshore in the early 1920s.

The "Empress" and Row Bay, Gareloch.

A view across the loch. The *Empress* can be seen in the background.

The parish church at Row (Rhu) in the early 1900s.

"ARDENCONNEL", C.H.A.GUEST HOUSE, RHU, HELENSBUR

Ardenconnel House, which for a time was a guest house. It as now been converted into flats.

The parish church at Rhu in a photograph taken in the early 1930s.

The Avenue, leading to Ardenconnel House.

Cumberland Terrace, *c.*1911.

The School Road.

Another picture of the *Empress*. The Ferry Inn and Rosneath Pier can be seen in the background.

The road along the loch, approaching the village from Helensburgh.

A view of Rhu village in a postcard from the early twentieth century.

Opposite: A view across the loch. The entrance to the pier can be seen at the bottom of Ardenconnel Road.

Ardenconnel Road, Row

A romantic postcard of a sunrise on the loch, c.1911.

Opposite above: The shore road during the 1900s.

Opposite below: Approaching the village from the south.

Helensburgh, Row Pier and Gareloch

A view across the Gareloch.

Opposite above: A view across the bay. Rosneath Castle can just be seen in the background.

Opposite below: The pier in the early 1920s.

Above: Mr MacDonald's house was originally called Rowaleyn. Perhaps because of the stigma attached to the house, the next occupant changed the name to Invergare.

Opposite above: The village from the loch.

Opposite below: In 1854, James Smith, the well-known Glasgow-based architect, built an imposing country house at Rhu. He left Rhu after the scandal of his daughter's (Maggie) murder case. The picture shows Mr and Mrs MacDonald and their son. They lived in the house from the early 1900s until 1922.

Another view of Invergare looking west.

Opposite above: Shandon Pier.

Opposite below: Shandon church from the pier.

Shandon Pier from the Shore Road.

Mr T. Grieve, the station master, at Shandon Station with Mr Thompson.

Shandon Station. One of the hillside stations about which a disgruntled passenger wrote in the *Railway Herald*: 'Sound heart and lungs and experience in hill climbing are essential to a man who hurries from the breakfast table to catch a train at one of the lochside stations. It is easier to go to the pier.'

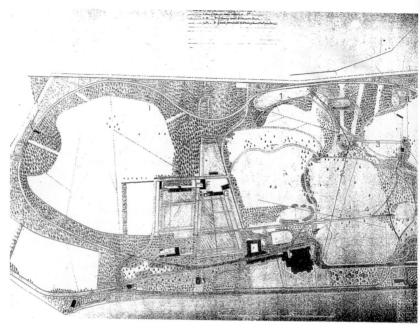

Above: The plan of West Shandon as it was built by Robert Napier.

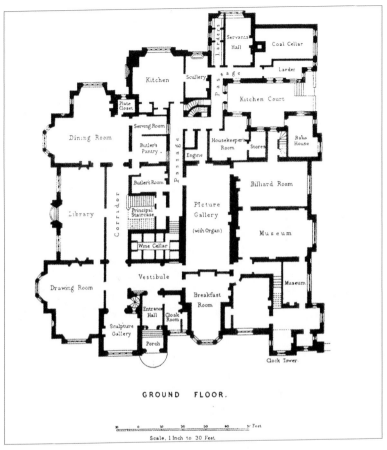

GROUND FLOOR.

Scale, 1 Inch to 30 Feet

Above: Plan of West Shandon.

Opposite below: Seventeen large houses were built at Shandon. The most impressive, West Shandon House, was built for Robert Napier, the eminent shipbuilder and engineer. From 1833, he had a summer cottage at Shandon and, by 1846, he took up permanent residence, building for himself and his family a majestic home on the site of the smaller cottage. By 1852, the house accommodated Napier's extensive collection of valuable antiques and paintings. David Livingston, the explorer, a close friend of Napier's, would bring him plants collected on his travels. As a result, the grounds and gardens were very impressive. After Napier's death in 1876, the house and its contents were sold for £38,000. It was bought by a company who enlarged it and ran it as a successful Hydropathic Establishment, advertised as providing: 'Russian, Turkish and Salt water swimming baths, covered and open tennis courts.' Additionally, a golf course, croquet and bowling green were available to patrons, all this for 18 shillings a day!

Shandon Hydropathic Establishment Gareloch

17912 *Will write in a day or two*

Shandon Hydropathic Hotel.

The imposing facade of the hotel.

Part of the hotel dining room.

The first lounge at the Shandon Hydropathic.

The second lounge at the Shandon Hydropathic.

Part of the Shandon Hydros extensive grounds.

The Shandon Hydro golf course.

Playing around on the Hydros golf course.

The fishing pond at the Hydro. The pond is still visible although somewhat overgrown now. Until recently, it was regularly used by the Helensburgh Model Boat Society, a use that Mr Napier would have probably approved of.

The Swan Pond in the Hydros grounds.

TARIFF

The inclusive terms are as follows—

APRIL TO SEPTEMBER – from 18/- per day
OCTOBER TO MARCH – from 15/- per day

and these terms include—

Bedroom, attendance, lights, Breakfast, Luncheon, Afternoon Tea, Dinner—also the enjoyment of Baths (private or swimming in Baths Department), Putting Green, Tennis on covered or open-air hard courts, Bowls, Croquet, Dancing in the Hotel Ball Room, Concerts, Entertainments.

Apart from the inclusive terms quoted above, the general tariff is as under—

APARTMENTS—Single Bedroom 8/6 to 15/-; Double 18/- to 36/-; Single Room, per day 25/-

BREAKFASTS—Plain 2/6, Table d'Hote 4/-
LUNCHEON—Table d'Hote 4/-
TEAS—Afternoon, in Lounge, 1/6
TEA IN BEDROOM, 1/-
DINNERS—Table d'Hote 7/6
DINNER AND DANCE—11/6.
MEALS IN BEDROOM—Extra per meal, 1/- per head.
VISITORS' SERVANTS—15/- per day, apartments and board.
GARAGE—Per week from 12/6 to 17/6; per day, 2/- to 3/-; 2 hours or less, 1/-. Motor Cycles and Side-cars, 2/- per day. Private Lock-up per week, £1/2/6; per day, 3/6. Washing cars, 2/6 to 5/-.

The very reasonable charges for the Hydro, or so they seem now.

The road to Garelochhead at Rowmore in an early twentieth-century postcard.

Opposite above: The pier in the picture was built in 1879, replacing a much older one that was eventually demolished in 1881. The older pier, which was built by McFarlane of Faslane in 1845, was the scene of the infamous 'Battle of Garelochhead Pier' one August Sunday in 1853. The local laird, James Colquhoun, disapproved of Sunday sailings and, with the help of some local people, barricaded the pier in an attempt to prevent the PS Emperor from berthing. The laird lost the day after a determined challenge from the steamer's crew. This picture was taken in 1909.

Oppozite below: The village of Garelochhead straddles the boundary between the ancient parishes of Row (Rhu) and Rosneath in a postcard from the 1910s. The village has changed little over the years apart from the housing development on the slopes of Feorlinbreck. During the 1850s, six different steamers called at the pier.

Garelochhead.

This picture, taken in 1920, shows Fernbreck. The railway viaduct can be seen in the background.

The Shore Road looking south.

The village from the hills to the west.

The motor launch *Thistle* on the loch in 1920.

The Smithy, Garloch Head.

A picture of the smithy at Garelochhead, taken in 1904. The smithy was just off Whistlefield Brae and was situated down a road that is now a private road.

The village viewed from the pier.

A holiday home in the village, in a picture taken in 1912.

A 1925 postcard of the village looking south.

The village from the shore.

The village from the station, 1906.

Looking north along Shore Road, 1906.

General view of the village, looking north, 1907.

Looking west from the station.

Fernicary.

This upturned boat was the home of two 'travelling folk', Jimmy and Susie Reid. Covered in oilskin and canvas it turned out to be a permanent home for the pair. Jimmy was a fisherman who sold his catch locally. After his death, Susie grew her own vegetables and worked as a domestic to supplement her income. She also had postcards of herself published to sell to tourists. It became a tradition with her to sell oranges at Garelochhead on New Years Day. She was in her seventies when she died. Her home, which was known as 'Susie's Castle', was burned down to prevent occupation by vagrants.

Susie's castle.

Whistlefield, Loch Long.

This picture taken in 1904 shows the hotel at Whistlefield. Loch Long and the entrance to Loch Goil can be seen in the background.

The cottages at Garelochhead; little changed over the years.

Whistlefield in 1913.

A 1906 postcard of Whistlefield.

Garelochhead to Coulport

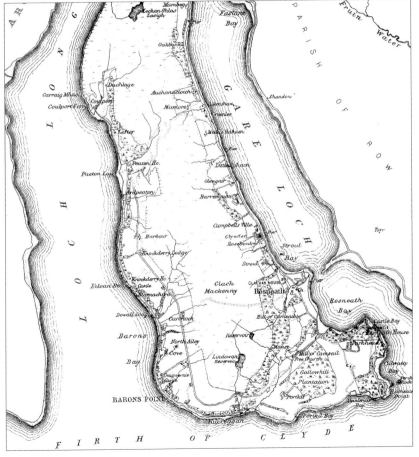

The parish of Rosneath.

Shore Road, Garelochhead.

CLYNDER ROAD, RAHANE

Rhane looking south.

Hattonburn.

Two brothers, Gruer and Ewing McGruer, opened their first boat yard at Rutherglen in November 1897. The boat-building yard at Hattonburn Clynder, which was originally Tait's boatyard, was bought by Ewing McGruer in 1910. Although no large yachts had been built at the yard, it had all the facilities Ewing McGruer and his four sons required. The family moved by puffer. On arriving in the Gareloch, the skipper of the *Urchin* simply ran aground at Hattonburn to make it easy for the McGruers to move their household effects ashore. The family lived in Braeside.

McGruers yard at Clynder.

Above and opposite, top: McGruers yard, Clynder. From the 1920s to the early 1970s, McGruers did much to encourage yachting in the local area. They hosted the Schools Week for the Mudhook Yacht Club and their 'corrugated iron' canteen, the old church, provided many a meal for the young sailors.

Opposite below: Ms Ella Stirling, standing at the gates of McGruers Clynder yard. The motor cruiser to the right is the *Maori*.

Above: In 1983, all the equipment from the Clynder yard was moved to Rosneath and the Clynder yard was sold to housing developers. This photograph was taken in 1986.

Opposite below: The northern end of the village. The pier can be seen at the extreme right of the picture. In 1876, the owner of Barreman House and Estate, Mr Robert Thom, probably with potential leases in mind, decided to build his own pier just to the north of the small village of Clynder. Barreman Pier boasted a large waiting room and crane. Despite the closeness of the two piers, local opposition and the somewhat ludicrous fact that, in spite of the piers being only 500 yards apart, steamers called at them both, the Barreman Pier gradually won the lions share of the passengers. It was, in fact, better built and had safer approaches than its southern rival. The pier was finally closed in September 1942 when military use of the loch finally caused the steamer companies to withdraw the service.

Above: Clynder from the loch, 1960.

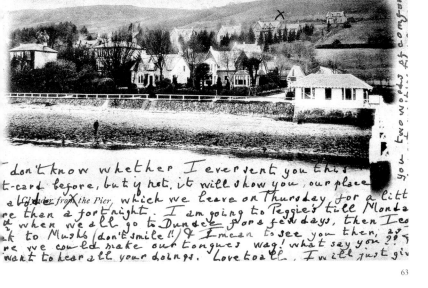

Clynder from the Pier.

don't know whether I ever sent you this
t-card before, but if not, it will show you, our place
re then a fortnight. I am going to Peggie's till Monda
d when we all go to Dundee for a few days, then I co
k to Musk (don't smile!!) & I mean to see you then, a
re we could make our tongues wag! what say you? go
want to hear all your doings. Love to all. I will just giv

you two words of comfort

Arthur Paynes shop, now the Old Manse Gallery. The 'iron church' can be seen in the background. It was later moved to McGruers' Hattonburn yard to be used as a canteen.

The Clynder Hotel seen in 1908.

Shore Road, Stroul, Rosneath.

The Shore Road at Stroul.

This picture, *c.*1906, shows Clachan House, built for the Factor of the Duke of Argyll. It stood where Rosneath primary school now stands.

The Clachan, Rosneath.

Above: The telegraph pole in the above picture is alongside the old post office. In the background is the horse and milk cart belonging to McIntyre of Little Rhane, who delivered daily. Each day, the horse would drink from the Stroul well at the foot of the brae.

Right: The Clachan, 1932.

The Clachan in the early 1900s. The photograph shows the smiddy and the grocery shop of David Silver. David's son, James, went on to own the local boat yard.

The Clachan.

In 1867, Archibald McKellar owned the boat yard at Rosneath, and he later opened another yard at Killcreggan which is known as 'McKellars Slipway'. He sold the Rosneath yard in 1889 to Roy William, who in 1891 sold it again to Peter McLean. McLean was more of an entrepreneur than a boat builder, and, by 1906, had sold the yard to Captain William Davidson. McLean then bought the Clynder Hotel. By this time, James Silver, who had served his apprenticeship under McLean, had left the Rosneath yard and was planning to set up business on his own. He had several commissions to build boats, particularly a 50ft cruiser for Alexander Kennedy, the founder of the Castlebank Dyeworks. James Silver was born in the Clachan Farm Cottage. His father, David Silver, was the local grocer and baker. In the spring of 1909, Captain Davidson committed suicide; his sons carried on for a short while but the yard went up for sale in May 1909. James Silver joined forces with John McCallum, a well-known yacht designer, and bought the yard. James Silver had established himself as a builder of fine yachts, but unfortunately, by keeping his prices low the yard ran up debts and, by 1914, the yard went into voluntary liquidation. It was taken over by Ferguson and Thompson Ltd of Glasgow, a chandlers and brokerage firm. They kept the name Silver and also kept James Silver on as manager. Not long after this, the yard advertised for a yacht designer and the successful candidate was John Bain. In 1916, James Silver left the yard and John Bain was promoted to manager. Under Bains' direction the Silvers yard prospered. He left the yard in 1957 and undoubtedly Silvers' success was largely due to this temperamental but workaholic man. He was known to the yard workforce as 'Hurricane Jack of the Vital Spark' and it was said that the staff could tell what sort of day they were going to have in the yard by the speed John Bain walked into the yard. The company was voluntarily wound up in July 1971. Since then the yard has changed hands several times. The present owners are keeping the memories alive by naming their company Silvers Marine Limited.

The Rosneath yard just after it was bought by James Silver.

John Bain and his wife, Jean.

Princess Louise always opposed the siting of the sign on top of the boat shed. Before it was finally positioned in 1939, John Bain had Mr Haig, the yard manager, to the pier to ensure that the Princess caught the ferry at the start of her trip to London. Once it had been confirmed she had left, the sign was hoisted into place.

By the mid-1930s, Silvers employed some 100 people. With these workers' welfare in mind, Silvers built a block of flats at the back of the yard and, not surprisingly, named them Silverhills. The photograph shows the flats being constructed.

General view of the yard.

A worker is putting the finishing touches to a boat.

The yard work force in the 1920s.

Mr W. Flemming in the paint shop.

Right: Finishing touches being put to the wheelhouse.

Below: The *Silver Trident* was the largest yacht built by Silvers. She cost £235,000 and took over two years to build.

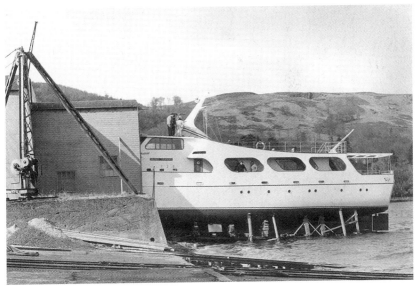

The men behind the *Silver Trident* are, from left to right: Mr Douglas Haig, works manager, Mr John Boyd, managing director, Mr Gordon Tran, designer and director.

The launch of the motor yacht *Thelma*.

Right: The crew smile while a lady officially launches the motor yacht *Thelma*.

Below: The motor yacht *Azure*.

The motor yacht *Silver Joy* on trials in the Gareloch.

The after deck of the *Silver Joy*.

Above and below: The deck saloon of the *Silver Joy* and (below) the master bedroom.

The motor yacht *Feldor*. She was built for Uniros Inc. Panama and launched from the Rosneath yard on 22 June 1959.

The deck saloon of the *Feldor*, looking forward.

The deck saloon of the *Feldor*, looking aft.

The wheelhouse.

The double cabin.

The covered side-deck of the 81ft yacht.

The Anchorage, Rosneath. The house stands just to the west of the boat yard and was built by John Bain for himself and his wife during the 1930s. Anyone who is familiar with the house will notice that the archway to the left of the house has now been removed. When John Bain left the yard, it was noticed that the house actually encroached the land owned by the yard. The new owners were willing to give Mr Bain the narrow strip of land, but rather than accept a favour from his former employer, he pulled down the trespassing brickwork.

A view from the landing showing the door to the guest bedroom. The compass rug was made by John Bains sister.

The lounge.

The living room: the sideboard is made of Japanese oak. During the building of the house, rumours circulated the yard that Mr Bain had used material from the yard. At one stage, he had all the bills associated with the house pinned on the works notice board to disprove these slanderous gossips.

A view across Rosneath towards the narrows, in a picture taken in 1916.

St Modens church, Rosneath.

In 1955, Willie McGruer was approached by the MOD for advice on the location of a storage and maintenance facility for the Ham class inshore minesweepers. Although the Ministry preferred a site at Stranraer, the Rosneath site on the Gareloch was eventually chosen. The MOD took over the old American base and built the sheds there. McGruer & Co. were given the contract to manage it. At this time, McGruer became a base for thirty-six of these small ships.

Rosneath village.

The Manse, Rosneath.

The famous silver firs which were planted either side of the drive to the mansion, built by the Campbells of Carrick at Camsail. It is said they were amongst the first silver firs to be planted in Britain, which may account for them being 'named' Adam and Eve. It is said the trees were planted in the early 1600s; they were dead by 1959.

The Ferry Inn. Rosneath Pier can be seen on the left.

Opposite above: The original inn was a thatched single-storey building situated some 400 yards south of the present building. At the beginning of the nineteenth century the inn was rebuilt on its present site using stones from Camsail House, and other improvements were added between 1862 and 1893. In the 1890s, Princess Louise, then Marchioness of Lorne, considered the possibility of living there herself and she commissioned Sir Edwin Lutyens, who was responsible for the present building. However, she moved to the Clachan and later to the Castle. The inn was combined with a hostel which was occupied by wounded soldiers from the South African War. The sign which hung over the door was said to have been painted by the Princess. The inn was requisitioned by the government in 1939. After the War it was used as married quarters and later sold in March 1958. Princess Louise was born in 1848, the sixth child of Queen Victoria. She married the Marquess of Lorne, who succeded as the Duke of Argyll in 1900, at St Georges Chapel, Windsor Castle on 21 March 1871. She had no children. She was the first royal allowed to marry a 'commoner'.

Opposite below: Outside the Ferry Inn.

Rosneath Pier; could this be the ferry?

The original castle was on the lochside in Castle Bay. It was destroyed by fire in 1802. The 5th Duke of Argyll replaced it with the pictured mansion in 1806. The new castle was designed by Joseph Bonomi, whose Italian origins are more than evident in the final design. The house was sold on the death of Princess Louise in 1939. It was used as a headquarters for the American forces based in Rosneath during the Second World War. After the War it was abandoned and eventually demolished up in 1961.

The impressive facade of the castle at night.

HRH Princess Louise with Troop and County Scout Pipe Band at the castle in 1934.

The 'Old Smithy' post Office at Rosneath.

Most of the photographs of Rosneath Castle were taken in its latter years. This photograph, taken from across Stroul Bay, gives some idea of what an imposing and majestic building it must have been in its prime.

During the early 1950s, the castle was left to deteriorate as caravans started moving in.

The Corn Mill at Rosneath. Its remains can still be seen halfway down the hill on the left.

Portkil House.

Old Kilcreggan.

Kilcreggan was originally a series of small farms and cottages dependent on a ferry service to Rosneath. With the arrival of the steamers the village expanded as feus were taken. This picture shows the village and the pier.

West End Villas, in 1907.

The delightful chapel is now the site of the Kilcreggan garage. It was built in 1869 by Francis Morton of Liverpool and was known locally as the 'iron church'.

Above: The initial feus at Kilcreggan were taken along the shore road. As the village grew, further roads were built on the hillside.

Opposite above: The first Kilcreggan Pier was built in 1850 and described as a 'most substantial pier with commodious waiting rooms and other conveniences similar to Rosneath'. It was initially served by steamers on the Holy Loch, Loch Long and Loch Goil route from Gourock. Alexander and John McLeod Campbell and their nephew 'Captain Bob' (P&A Campbell, or 'white-funnelled steamers') sold the goodwill of their trade to the Caledonian Railway Company; Kilcreggan Pier became the focus of a three pointed race between the various railway companies. There are many stories of the steamers racing for the pier in order to land their passengers first. It may have been due to this waterborne rivalry that the pier had to be rebuilt; the new pier was duly opened on 25 September 1897. The steamers were eventually withdrawn at the end of the 1933 season. The buildings were renewed and the pier structure strengthened in 1964. It is the only traditional pier that remains open all year round on the Clyde.

Opposite below: The initial feus were taken up on the Shore Road, then, as more land was required, a higher road was built. These tenement blocks, opposite the pier, were built between 1888 and 1903.

THE PIER, KILCREGGAN   B 9883

Inverclyde House with its splendid gardens.

Cove parish church.

Cove Pier opened in 1852. It was built primarily to encourage feuars and, despite its rare exposed position, being at the mercy of the Clydes well-known 'soun' westerlies', attracted a fair number of potential house owners.

The foreshore at Cove.

Kilcreggan Chapel, now the site of the garage.

Cove and Kilcreggan Guides, 1938. The picture shows, from left to right: Sandie Lee, Mary Alison, Capt. R. Hunter, Rennie Jardine, Anne Sutherland.

Opposite above: Cove village from Baron Point.

Opposite below: An evening on the foreshore at Cove. From left to right: Mr McPherson, Joe MacAdam, Jim Sutherland, Jim Gurthrie, John Alison. This picture was taken in 1935.

Right: John Alison, the first pier master at Cove.

Apart from being pier master, Mr Alison also found time to run a fishing business. He is seen here while mending his nets.

Coronation Parade at Kilcreggan in 1953.

Will Richardson's shop at Cove. The Alisons lived in the flat above the shop.

Richardson's shop just after the fire which totally destroyed it. The site is now the Cove Fire Station.

Left: Mary Alison on the beach at Cove.

Below: Going for a car ride at Cove during the 1930s.

Opposite above: Cove village.

Opposite below: A 1950s postcard from Kilcreggan.

Cove Village (5

THE PIER

KILCREGGAN

SILVER BAY

FROM EAST

VIEW FROM ABOVE KILCRE

KILCREGGAN

FROM WATER

COVE FROM NORTH AILEY

203616

A photograph of the staff of the Coulport Torpedo range.

Cragdarroch Cove in the 1920s.

The foreshore at Cove.

Inverclyde and Craigrownie castles from the loch.

Lidden church.

Letter Cottage, Coulport.

The searchlight battery at Cove during the Second World War.

A postcard from Cove sent during the 1920s.

Above and below: Coulport House.

A wedding reception at the Clevedon Hotel, Cove.

Looking over Portkil, towards the Clyde.

Arddeaton, Cove.

Pearl Ware: in a picture from the late 1800s showing members of the McMorran family.

Mrs M. McMorran's mother, who married John Alison, the grandson of John Alison who came from Skye to be the first pier master at Cove.

Public hall and UF church at Cove.

Cove Village in the early 1900s.

Hartfield House, Cove.

The entrance to Inverclyde, Cove.

Heathfield House, Kilcreggan.

Cove Pier, built in 1852 to encourage feuars. The first houses were built around the landing place.

Glen Eden Cove.

AERIAL VIEW. COVE

An aerial view of Cove taken in 1921: the pier can clearly be seen.

Ferry Cottage, Coulport.

An aerial view of Coulport: the unusual house on the left is effectively a Swiss chalet and was built by George Boucher (the designer of Coulport House, on the bottom right) for himself. The house was pulled down prior to the building of the armaments depot at Coulport during the early 1960s.

Above and below: Coulport House.

A walk at Coulport.